New Patterns from OLD ARCHITECTURE

New *Patterns* — from — O L D ARCHITECTURE

Carol Wagner

Photography by Howard Wagner and Charley Lynch

American Quilter's Society

P. O. Box 3290 • Paducah, KY 42002-3290

Wagner, Carol.
    New Patterns from old architecture: Carol Wagner: photography by Howard Wagner and
Charley Lynch.
    p. cm.
        Includes bibliographical references and index.
        ISBN 0-89145-840-9
        1. Appliqué--patterns. 2. Patchwork--patterns 3. Quilting--patterns. 4. Decoration and
ornament, architectural --themes, motives. 5. Architecture, Victorian--themes, motives.
        I. Title.TT779.W33 1995   95-11618
        746.44'5--dc20   CIP

Additional copies of this book may be ordered from:

American Quilter's Society
P.O. Box 3290
Paducah, KY 42002-3290
@12.95. Add $2.00 for postage and handling

Printed by IMAGE GRAPHICS, INC., Paducah, Kentucky

DEDICATION

To Howard
For his help, his encouragement, and for just being there.

A C K N O W L E D G M E N T S

There are several people who deserve a special thank you; my husband, Howard, who always carries a camera at his side;

my sister, Phyllis Mittelstadt, who insisted I had to see the floor in the public library;

Lael Eggington, who loaned me the piece of walnut molding;

Hibbing High School's office staff and stage manager, for their time and assistance;

and St. Luke's Catholic Church in St. Paul, Minnesota.

CONTENTS

Quiltmakers receive the inspiration for their quilt patterns from just about every imaginable source. During the show and tell portion of many quilt meetings I have attended, a quilter will tell of being inspired by a photo in a magazine or an illustration in a book. Sometimes a greeting card received for Valentine's Day, Mother's Day, Christmas, or Hanukkah inspired her quilt design. Autumn's colorful foliage has given rise to many leaf patterns. Even vacation photographs have been re-created in splendid pictorial wall quilts. Quilters are resourceful and clever individuals!

In much the same manner, architectural gingerbread decorating the interiors and exteriors of old buildings can be an excellent source for quilt patterns. For years I have been fascinated with Victorian era buildings in our country. Every surface seems to be lavishly decorated with ornate carvings, tiles, and moldings. The manner in which flowers, leaves, vines, and animal forms were used to create the elaborate ornamentation embellishing these structures intrigues me. It is fun to explore and prowl through historic buildings, landmarks, and churches just to look for designs to use in a quilt. In fact, several years ago while in a major Midwestern city, I attended an antique show held in a newly restored century old landmark. This was no ordinary antique show. Included in the exhibitors' displays were valuable Imari bowls, authentic Paul Revere silver pieces, costly Oriental rugs, and European furniture well over 250 years old.

Many prospective customers were prominent people from other states who came specifically to attend this prestigious show. While others were looking at these elegant and very expensive antiques, I was on my hands and knees examining the inlaid designs in the wood floor and the carved moldings. I was glad neither my husband nor adult children were accompanying me because they surely would have denied even knowing me, much less being related to me!

Over the years my fascination with architectural gingerbread grew. I became aware that much of it could be adapted into block and border patterns for our quilts. Sometimes I think my interest increases for this purpose, to look for more designs, to photograph them, to make sketches and doodles and finally, to convert them into quilt patterns.

Some quilters enjoy adapting these designs and patterns themselves, but many do not. This book was written with the latter group in mind, and it provides them with a sampling of patterns based on architectural details. They can plunge right into the fun and nitty-gritty of cutting, snipping, and stitching blocks. Those quilters wishing to learn more about making their own patterns will find detailed instructions in my book, *Adapting Architectural Details for Quilts*.

New Patterns
from
Old Architecture

Chapter 1 How to Use the Patterns

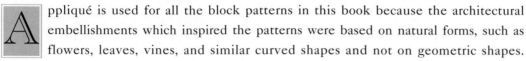

How to Use the Patterns

Appliqué is used for all the block patterns in this book because the architectural embellishments which inspired the patterns were based on natural forms, such as flowers, leaves, vines, and similar curved shapes and not on geometric shapes. These shapes are easiest to duplicate and stitch using appliqué. Most of the patterns in this book can be done by anyone having good basic to intermediate appliqué skills.

The block patterns are designed for a twelve-inch finished square, the size quilters have come to regard as a standard size for quilt blocks. This size provides the quiltmaker with many possibilities. Four, six, or nine blocks are enough to make a wallhanging or crib quilt, and twenty or more will make a bed quilt.

Each pattern is accompanied by a photograph of the actual architectural detail and a photograph of the appliquéd block adaptation. I share my thoughts about that particular design, why I selected it, and occasionally some of the problems I encountered and solved in the adaptation which may help you understand why certain elements of a design were omitted, enlarged, or otherwise changed. My goal was to simplify the design enough to make it easy to appliqué, but at the same time, not alter its appearance to any degree from the original architectural detail. The appliquéd block should resemble the pattern source.

The patterns are drawn full size. However, the limitations of page size may make it necessary to break up the pattern into sections, and the patterns need to be transferred from the book. A piece of lightweight or tracing paper placed over the pattern will allow you to trace it with comparative ease. You then can transfer the tracing to your favorite template material such as plastic, cardboard, or freezer paper. Generally, I do not recommend photocopying patterns from a book. The book will not lay flat on the copier glass and this will distort the pattern. If you want to photocopy a pattern, check with your local photocopy shop to determine the accuracy of its equipment. You may also find one or more of the following methods helpful in making templates from the patterns in the book.

Templates for Needle Turning

If your template plastic is translucent and allows you to see the pattern through it, simply trace the pattern directly from the book onto the plastic. Number or label the parts and cut them apart.

If your template plastic is too opaque to see through, you need to trace the pattern onto lightweight paper or tracing paper. Glue your traced drawing to a piece of template plastic using a glue stick or artist's mounting adhesive. Number or label each part of the drawing as it is shown in the book, and then cut the plastic apart and the templates are all set!

You will need a 12" square of tag board or other lightweight cardboard and a sheet of yellow dressmaker's carbon paper, only yellow, please! This paper has a waxy yellow coating on one side which will not leave marks on your appliqué fabric when you iron it around the pattern piece. Dressmaker's carbon can be found in the notions section of most fabric stores. Be sure the package contains waxy paper. The wax free does not work as well.

Tape the tag board square to a flat surface, and tape the drawing on top of it. Slide the dressmaker's carbon, waxy side down, between the drawing and the cardboard. Trace over the drawing, pressing down firmly with a pencil or stylus, and moving the carbon if necessary. Remove the tape, label the parts, and cut apart.

Most quilt shops now carry a heat-resistant plastic template material which can be used with a hot iron the same way as cardboard templates are used with spray starch. Plastic templates have the advantage of the edges retaining their shape, and if you use spray starch to shape the applique pieces, the plastic does not absorb the moisture and bend.

Transferring the Pattern onto Your Fabric

If the color of your foundation fabric is light enough to see through, the fabric and pattern can be taped to a flat surface and the pattern traced onto the fabric. If the foundation fabric is too dark for the pattern to show through, try using a piece of white dressmaker's carbon placed between the pattern and fabric. Use a stylus or dried-out ballpoint pen to trace the pattern. Also, a template of the pattern can be made and used to transfer the pattern to the foundation block fabric.

Several patterns in the book show only a quarter of the pattern. Make a template of the section, and divide your foundation block into quarters by folding. Find the center of your foundation fabric and place the center of the template on it. Rotate or reverse the template as necessary to trace the outline into each section of the fabric.

Figure 1
The background square was divided into quarters by folding. This template will mark each quarter.

For several reasons I suggest using a 13" square of fabric for your background or foundation block instead of the usual 12½" unfinished square. First, blocks can become pulled out of shape or distorted when appliqué stitches are pulled down securely. Some puckering might occur under the appliqué making the block too small.

Secondly, some fabrics, even the better quality goods, fray more than others. Recently I used a very good fabric from a well-known manufacturer as the background for a miniature wallhanging. As I appliquéd my pattern on it and started quilting, the outer edges frayed at an alarming rate. After losing more than ⅛" on each of the four sides, I panicked. The outer edges were dwindling away, and there would not be enough fabric to hold a binding! I finally had to dab a bit of anti-fray solution along the outer edges to hold the threads in place.

After completing the appliqué work and pressing the block, re-measure and cut it to the usual unfinished 12½" square. This assures you will have a square that fits against the lattice strip or adjoining block. If you are appliquéing a border, allow an extra inch in both width and length, and trim it later.

Quilting Stencils

We are accustomed to using commercial stencils made of plastic material, and although plastic is very durable, it can be difficult to cut. Being rather clumsy with a craft knife, I sometimes find it hard to control when applying the pressure needed to cut all the way through the plastic. Frequently, I cut my quilting stencil out of old, used file folders. This lightweight cardboard can be easily cut with sharp pointed scissors, and I tend to be more accurate with this material. The stencils retain their shape nicely even through repeated use on a project, particularly if you handle them carefully and store them flat in a box.

For a more durable stencil, I recommend plastic template material and cut it with scissors. If the pattern calls for an opening within the design, use a paper punch to make a few "starter" holes for the tip of the scissors or cut a slit in the plastic through a section of the pattern and cut out the area you need to remove. Seal the slit with transparent tape. Simple and safe!

A silhouette stencil is an outline of the pattern shape cut from the template material or cardboard. (Fig. 2.) These stencils can be held in position for marking the quilt top by weaving long quilt pins through the fabric and across the top of the stencil or by using bits of masking tape along the edges.

Figure 2
These are silhouette stencils.

Some of the stencil patterns are marked with zigzag lines with the letter "B" printed between them. These are bridges and needed to give stability to the stencil or to hold the stencil sections together, and they are not a part of the pattern itself. When you cut your stencil, you need to include the bridges. (Fig 3.) When quilting, stitch across the gap in your marking line just as you would with commercially produced stencils.

Some suggestions for quilting portions of the appliqué work have been offered and are indicated by dashes on the patterns. Please keep in mind these are only suggestions and not rules etched in stone. They represent ideas for portions of the pattern, particularly the leaves and flower petals, not for all of it. Quilt the blocks as you wish and have fun with them.

Figure 3
The bridges on these stencils are marked with a "B" and stabilize the parts of the stencil.

Block Patterns

Crest and Wreath

I always thought it would be fun to have a family coat of arms, but as a hobby genealogist, I have learned my German peasant ancestors did not have one, or at least none I have been able to find. When I discovered this crest and wreath design on the side of a building, I decided to adopt it as my own and to make an appliqué pattern for a quilt block. (Fig. 4.) Who knows, some day I may appliqué my initials or even a spool of thread and scissors on it.

I simplified the wreath by eliminating the scallop details, and by rounding the contours instead. The texture of leaves could be created by using a print fabric in the appliqué. I substituted a single band of fabric where the ribbons criss-crossed to make the appliqué easier. The ribbons on the architectural piece curl and hang down creating a vertical design. Since the pattern needed adjusting to fit into a square, I curled the ribbons toward the outer edges of the block making it fill a square quite nicely. (Fig. 5.)

The block is not difficult to appliqué, especially if you follow the construction hints given on the next page. Appliqué the pieces in numerical order as shown on the pattern.

Figure 4
This architectural embellishment was the inspiration for an appliqué pattern.

Figure 5
The Crest and Wreath quilt block looks very similar to the original design.

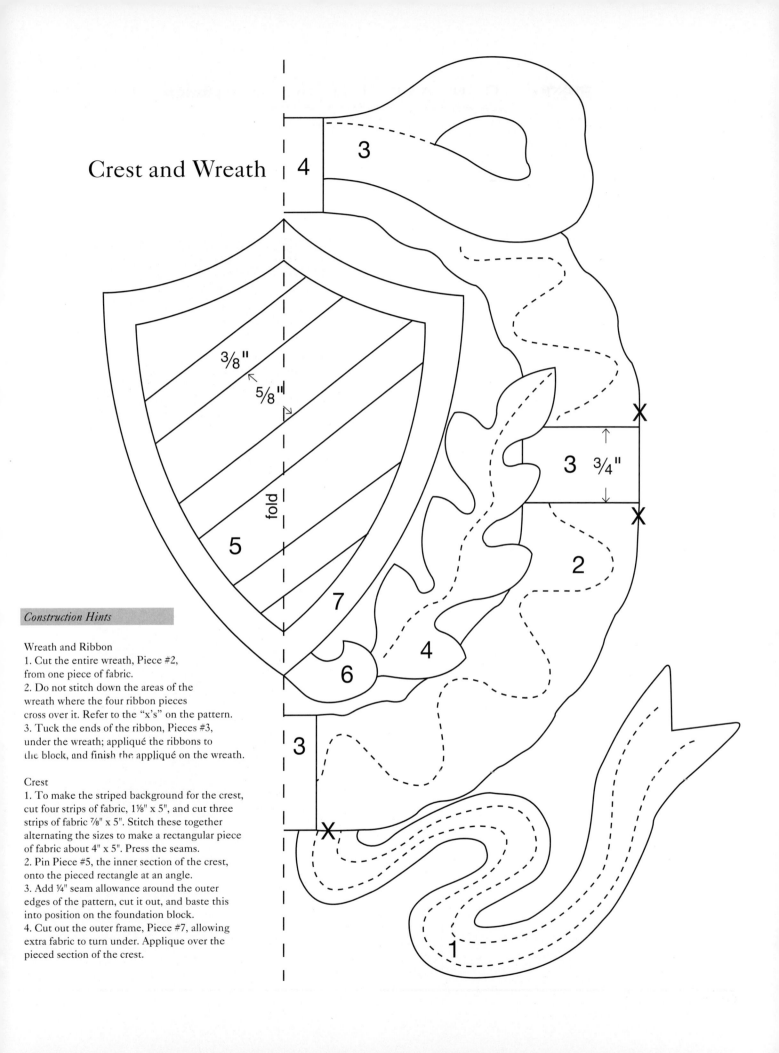

Crest and Wreath

4

3

3/8 "

5/8 "

fold

5

7

6

4

2

3 3/4 "

3

1

Construction Hints

Wreath and Ribbon
1. Cut the entire wreath, Piece #2, from one piece of fabric.
2. Do not stitch down the areas of the wreath where the four ribbon pieces cross over it. Refer to the "x's" on the pattern.
3. Tuck the ends of the ribbon, Pieces #3, under the wreath; appliqué the ribbons to the block, and finish the appliqué on the wreath.

Crest
1. To make the striped background for the crest, cut four strips of fabric, 1⅛" x 5", and cut three strips of fabric ⅞" x 5". Stitch these together alternating the sizes to make a rectangular piece of fabric about 4" x 5". Press the seams.
2. Pin Piece #5, the inner section of the crest, onto the pieced rectangle at an angle.
3. Add ¼" seam allowance around the outer edges of the pattern, cut it out, and baste this into position on the foundation block.
4. Cut out the outer frame, Piece #7, allowing extra fabric to turn under. Applique over the pieced section of the crest.

Berry Bush

I discovered this carved newel post in a county history center. An entire foyer and staircase had been salvaged from one of the city's Victorian mansions and had been moved to the history center as a permanent exhibit. Attracted by the warm golden color of the oak woodwork in this exhibit, I noticed two designs carved in the newel post. Serendipity! (Fig. 7.) While the design at the top of the post was quite large, the design below it was minuscule, probably not larger than a two-inch square, but definitely one to warrant close scrutiny. Although so tiny, it was already carved in a square shape design which would help greatly in making the drawing for a block pattern. The design could be used with little adaptation despite its petite size.

As I started to work with the design, I realized two parts of the design needed changing. The small leaf shapes and the stems of the larger corner leaves blended into the background of carved wood which can be done in a three-dimensional medium, but not with appliquéd fabric. An appliquéd fabric has a beginning and an end. The changes to the design were not difficult to make. I made the leafy shapes into four separate little leaves which could be appliquéd between the larger corner leaves, and extended the length of the stems so the ends could be tucked under the berries. (Fig. 7.)

This is an easy appliqué pattern and even beginners should have no problems. As the pattern is symmetric, only one quarter of it is shown. Refer to the pattern drawing for placement. Stitch in numerical order as shown.

Figure 6
A very tiny design was carved into a newel post.

Figure 7
Only a few changes were made in the original design to create this pattern.

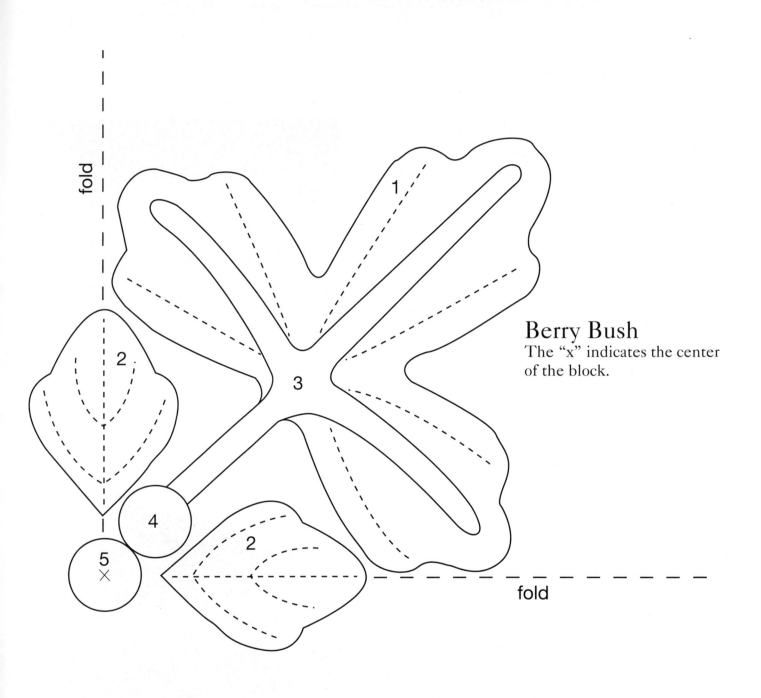

fold

fold

1

2

3

2

4

5
×

Berry Bush
The "x" indicates the center
of the block.

Orchid Corsage

his is the larger of the two designs carved into the newel post in the history center exhibit. The simplicity of the leaves and blossom indicated this would be a suitable appliqué design. The leaves and flower petals were large with smooth uncomplicated curves. (Fig. 8.) A quilter could hardly go wrong adapting this design. The only pattern change I made was to complete the shape of the two petals on the carving's lower edge and to add a fourth petal at the bottom. A beginning quilter could appliqué this pattern without difficulty. Appliqué in numerical order as shown.

Every pattern has to have a name. As I appliquéd this pattern, it reminded me of a single blossom corsage, perhaps an orchid, so I selected that as its name. (Figs. 8 & 9.)

With some minimal changes, this could be used as a quilting design, especially in those triangular areas created when blocks are set on point. To use this pattern for quilting, eliminate two leaves, Pieces #1 and 2, and remove the petal at the very bottom of the pattern. Reduce the height of the tallest petal by cutting the stencil on the line indicated. Figure 10 shows how the stencil should look when it is cut.

Figure 8
This is the larger of the two designs carved into the newel post.

Figure 9
Here is the pattern developed from the carving.

Figure 10
A quilting stencil was made from this pattern.

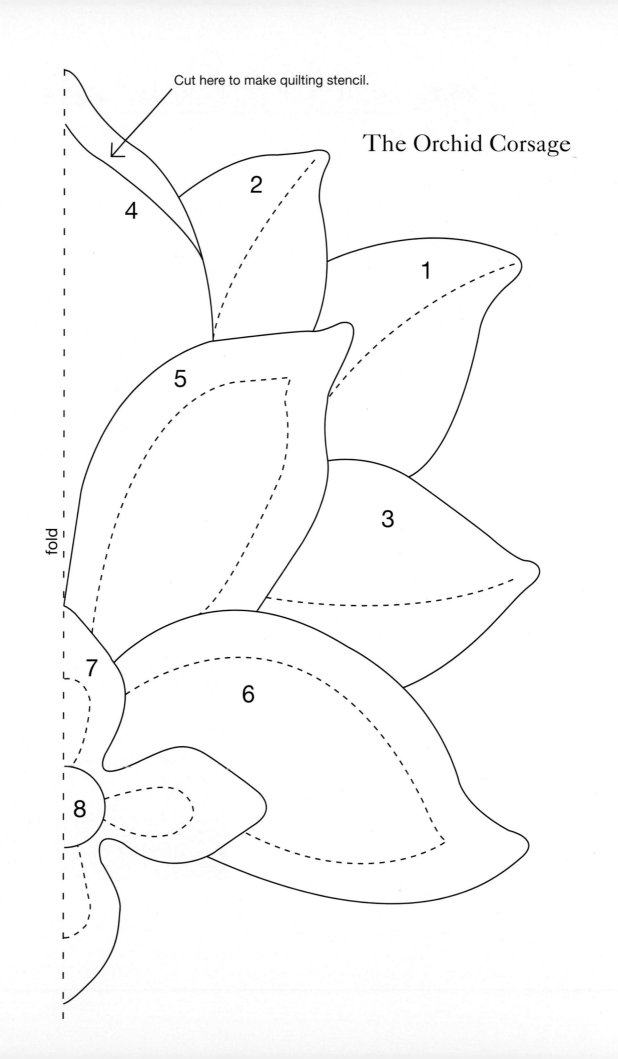

Cut here to make quilting stencil.

The Orchid Corsage

fold

2

4

1

5

3

7

6

8

Laurel Wreath

This ornamentation was located at an entrance of a Midwestern courthouse and included several designs suitable for adaptation to quilt patterns. The word Justice, written between two wreaths, was located in the stone panel over the main door. The wreath design was not too complex making it suitable for appliqué. Miniature quilts have become very popular and wouldn't this make a fine pattern for a Christmas wallhanging?

The only really necessary adaptation was adjusting the stems at the top of the wreath. Notice how the stem blends into the leaves on the right side of the wreath. (Fig. 12.) This cannot be done with fabric unless the quilter wants leaves and stem to be the same color. If I wanted to use different colors, I had to alter the design. I solved this problem by bringing both loops of the stems to the front of the wreath making it possible to use different colors for stems and leaves. Now the ends of the leaves would be hidden under the curves of the stems. (Fig. 11.)

Appliqué in numerical order as shown. All the berries can be stitched on last.

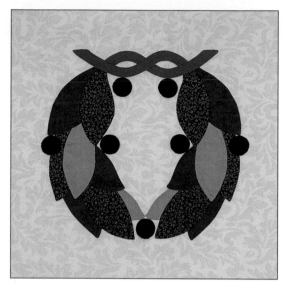

Figure 11
The Laurel Wreath pattern came from the architectural wreath design.

Figure 12
This wreath design was found on a courthouse.

Laurel Wreath

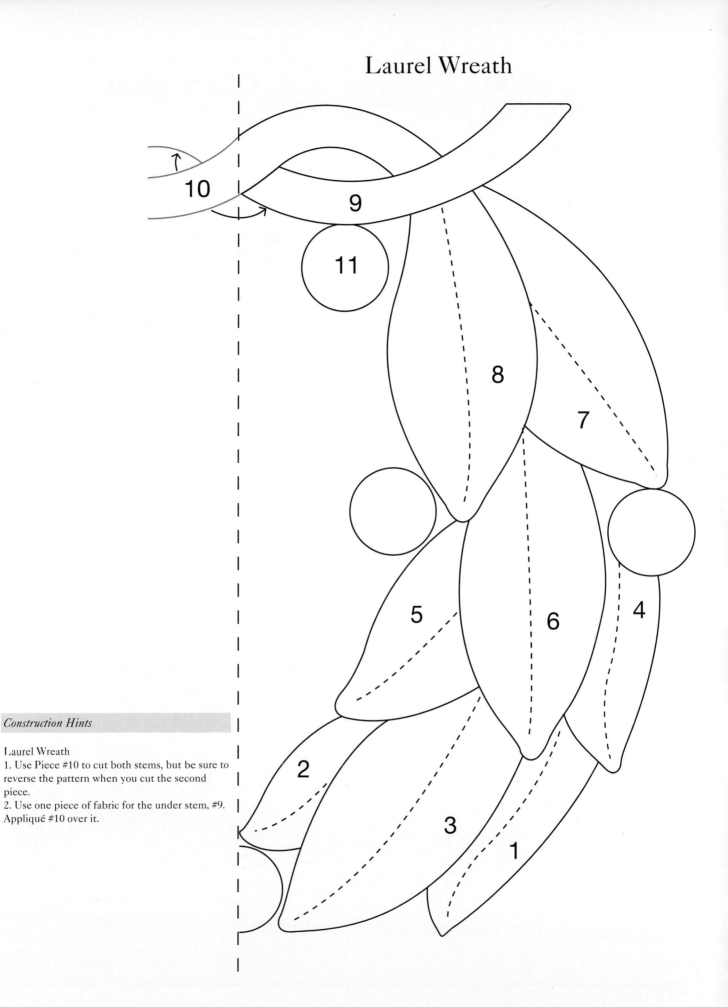

Construction Hints

Laurel Wreath
1. Use Piece #10 to cut both stems, but be sure to reverse the pattern when you cut the second piece.
2. Use one piece of fabric for the under stem, #9. Appliqué #10 over it.

The Bell

Several enormous stone or cast concrete bells decorate the exterior wall of an old building in downtown Milwaukee. I thought it odd this unusual and attractive gingerbread was located on the alley side of the building where it was not very noticeable. (Fig.13.) Perhaps over the years, the city just grew to surround this structure. I was overjoyed when I noticed the bells because of the wonderful appliqué pattern they would make. (Fig. 14.) Wouldn't it be fun to use this pattern for a Christmas quilt?

The upper section of the bell had to have several changes from the original piece of architecture. The large scrolls or curlicues which swoop from the top could not be cut from a single piece of fabric. The various ways I thought of to turn or manipulate the fabric to replicate the curl seemed just too complicated to be practical! After making several test patterns and trials, I changed the scrolls and curved them slightly so the quilter could make them either a part of the foliage, an additional ribbon, or simply another part of the design, according to whim.

The center section just above the bell had some fanciful leaves which I wanted to retain. To achieve this, I eliminated the sharpest curves and made the others a bit more gentle and less difficult to appliqué. Because the ribbons had too many folds and twists for easy appliqué, I removed some folds and replaced them with curves.

A beginner with some experience should not find this pattern too difficult despite the large number of curves. Appliqué in numerical order given.

Figure 13
The bell design was found on an outside wall of a building.

Figure 14
This quilt block pattern was inspired by the stone bell.

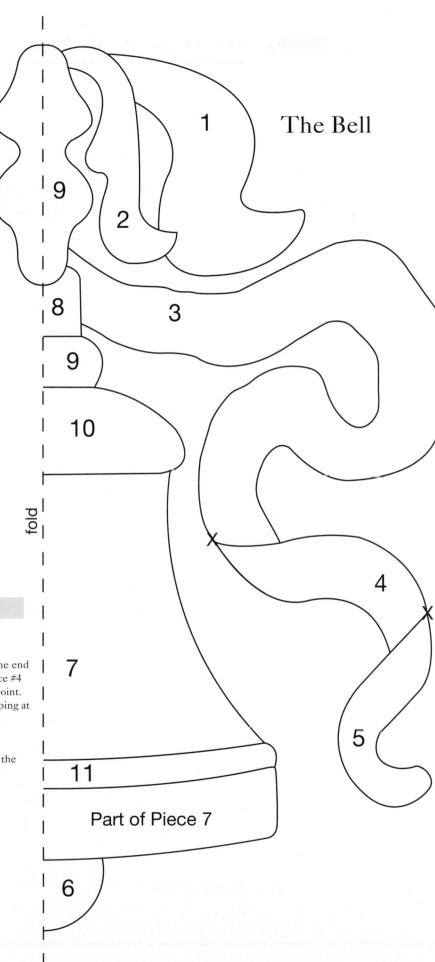

The Bell

fold

Construction Hints

Ribbon
1. Appliqué Piece #3 to the "x."
2. Tuck the end of the ribbon, Piece #4, under the end of Piece #3. Continue stitching, appliquéing Piece #4 over the end of Piece #3, eliminating the sharp point.
3. Using Piece #4, repeat the previous step, stopping at the "x" on Piece #4. Appliqué Piece #5.

Bell
1. Cut the main section of the bell, Piece #7 and the lower rim from one piece of fabric, no seam.
2. Appliqué the narrow band, Piece #11 over it.

Part of Piece 7

Rose Buds

One day while exploring old buildings in my community, I found this carved wood embellishment over a door inside a church. A kind custodian brought me a ladder so I could get a closer look and take a picture. The carving seemed to have some potential for appliqué if a few modifications were made. (Fig. 15.)

Figure 15
A carved design was located in a door frame inside a church.

A piece of wood can be carved to create the appearance of overlapping leaves, petals, or stems, but this cannot be achieved with a single flat piece of fabric. Fabric has only two dimensions, length and width. To give the illusion of depth, quilters can layer fabrics, change colors, use prints or textures. Because a small amount of fabric is needed on the appliqué edge for turning under as it is stitched in place, I could not adapt this design so it could be cut from a single piece of fabric. This small amount of fabric loss "eats" up some of the design, reducing its size and enlarging any slits or notched edges. To achieve the appearance of overlapping, I had to change or open the design so several pieces of fabric could be used. This made the pattern look like flower buds set against a background of leaves. Although the adapted pattern no longer resembled the original wood piece as much as I would have liked, I was still rather pleased with the result. (Fig. 16.) Perhaps if this pattern were appliquéd in several shades of the same color, such as green, it would look more like the original.

This pattern should not be too difficult for an experienced beginner. Appliqué in the order as shown. Refer to the pattern for placement.

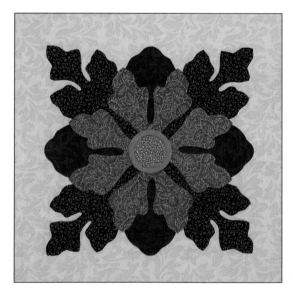

Figure 16
The Rose Buds block was adapted from the wood carving.

Rose Buds

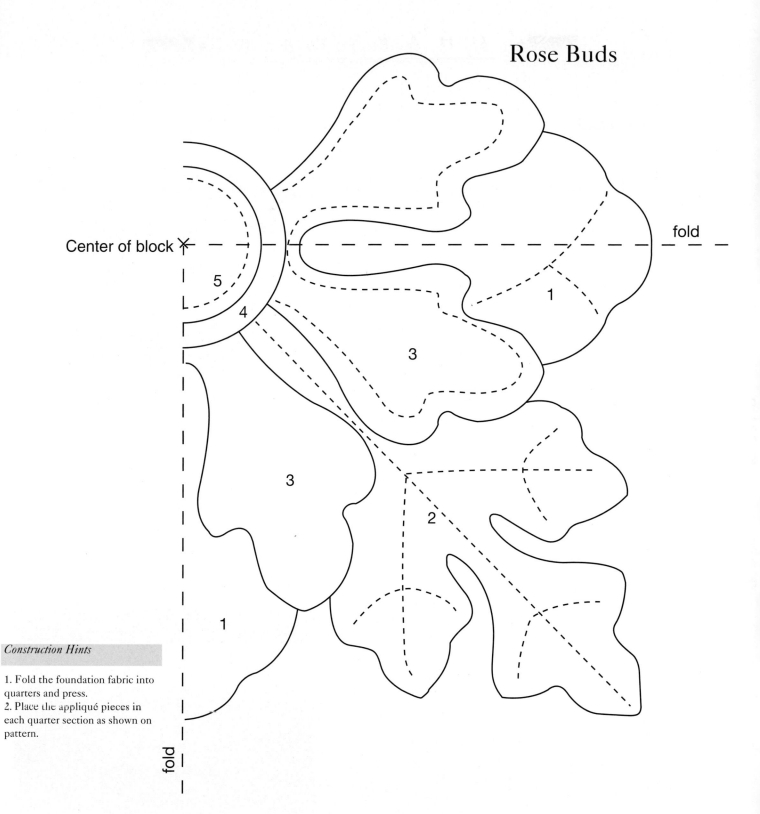

Center of block ✗ — — — — — — — — — — — — — fold

5

4

3

1

3

2

1

fold

Construction Hints

1. Fold the foundation fabric into quarters and press.
2. Place the appliqué pieces in each quarter section as shown on pattern.

Pitt's Heart

O n a recent trip to Pittsburgh, we discovered an elaborate gingerbready building in one of the most heavily trafficked areas of the city. Taking photographs would be literally a life or death decision. It would involve trying to set up the tripod and snapping the picture during the red light interval of the traffic signals. We could not return to this location at a better time of day, so my husband quickly stepped into the street with his camera only to discover he had to shoot into a bright sunny sky. Sometimes you just have to seize the moment, shoot the picture, run, and hope for the best!

Because of the quality of the photograph, adaptation to the bottom of this ornamentation piece was too difficult, so I made it look the way I wanted it to look. (Fig. 18.) I liked the overall heart shape with the flowers and simplified that part of the design. Since the bottom section of the architectural detail was not very clear on our photo, I just notched the ends of the design at the base of the heart to make them look like ribbons. (Fig. 17.)

Appliqué in numerical order.

Figure 17
Some of the original details were used and others were omitted in the Pitt's Heart pattern.

Figure 18
The two heart-shaped embellishments are located near the roof of the building.

Pitt's Heart

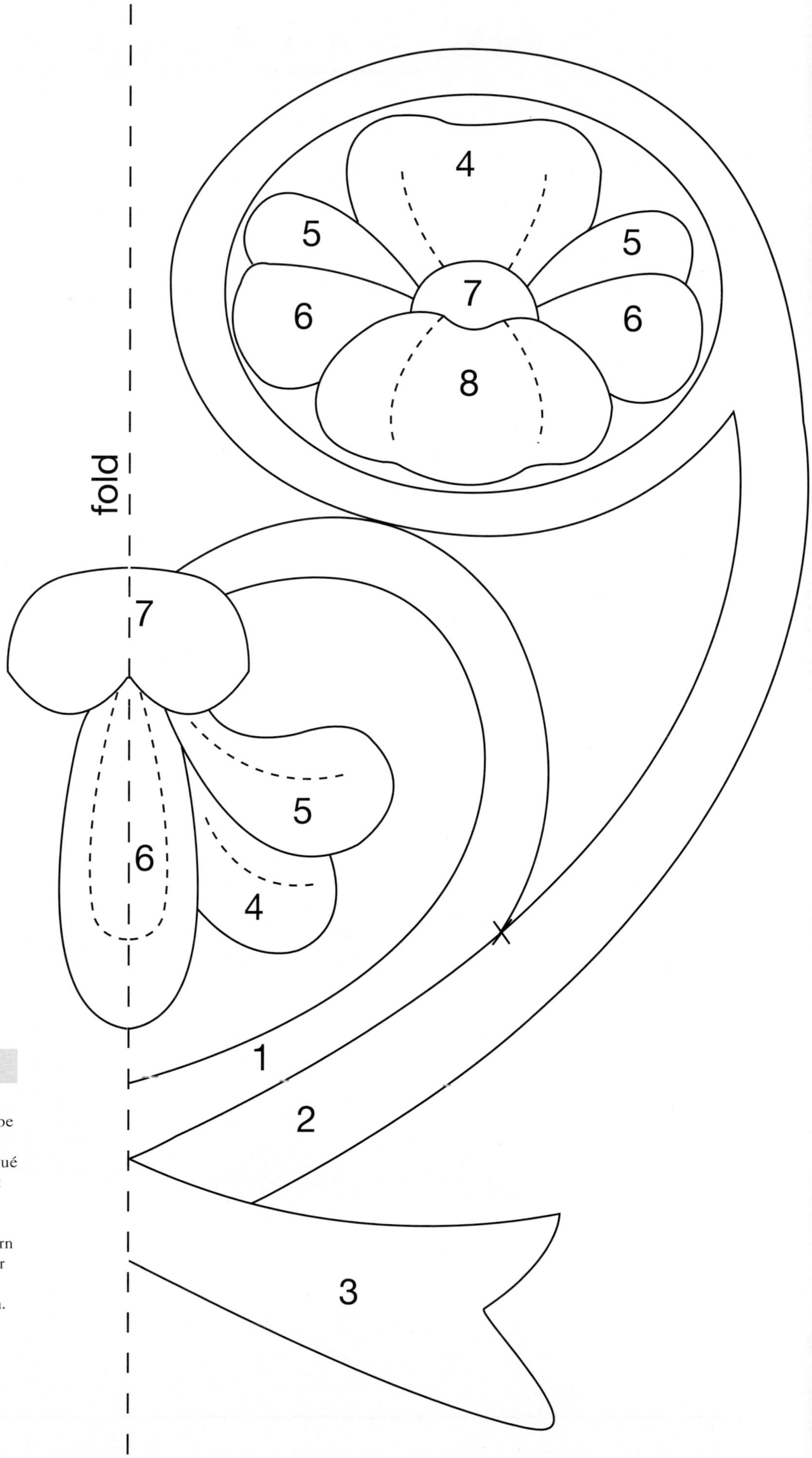

fold

4

5   5

6   6

7

8

7

5

6

4

X

1

2

3

Construction Hints

1. Use Piece #2 for both pieces of the heart, but be sure to reverse your template when you cut the second piece. It doesn't matter which you appliqué first, just as long as one piece crosses the other at the bottom.
2. Mark the stitching line on Pieces #1 and #2.
3. Cut a slit at the "x" on Piece #1, and do not turn under the section between the "x's" on the lower edge of this piece.
4. Appliqué both Piece #2's on top of this section.

Nebraska Windflower

The pattern for the Nebraska Windflower quilt block was developed from the tile design.

T hese floral designs were located on either side of the entrance to an old office building in Lincoln, Nebraska. The accumulated layers of paint and street dust obscured much of the fine detailing on the tiles. (Fig. 19.) Nonetheless, it is an attractive design and very appropriate for an appliqué pattern.

Only very small sections of the leaves were visible between the large flower petals. I wanted to expose more of them to add another color to the appliqué. Therefore, it was necessary to reduce the width of each petal to obtain more leaf. The center of the flower would be difficult to duplicate with fabric because it would involve lots of small pieces. After trying a few adaptations, which proved to be far, far more frustrating than fun, I decided to use two circles and the star shape for the center. (Fig. 20.)

I used reverse appliqué for the vein portion of the inner petals. Figure 21 shows what the template for a petal should look like. Appliqué in numerical order as shown.

Figure 20
Adaptations were made of the flower design on the tiles.

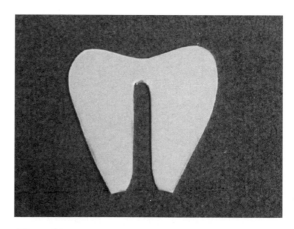

Figure 21
Template for Piece #3.

Nebraska Windflower

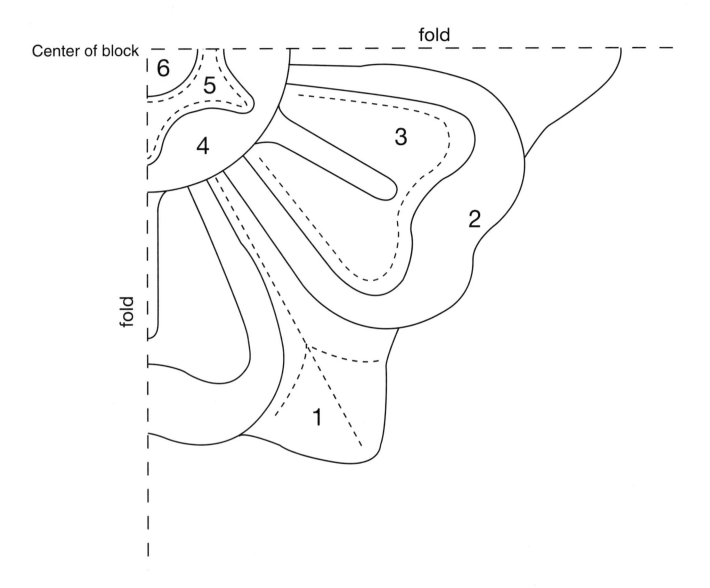

Center of block   fold

fold

6
5
4
3
2
1

Construction Hints

Petals
1. Appliqué petal piece #2 onto the block.
2. Cut out piece #3 and mark the vein; position this piece onto piece #2 and appliqué.
3. Cut a slit in the center of the vein, tuck under the edges, and stitch as for reverse appliqué.

Bavarian Plate

Figure 22
This architectural piece was unusual because of its octagonal shape.

W henever I go to another city I always look for architectural gingerbread. While visiting Milwaukee, Wisconsin, I spotted an octagonal shape near the top of a hotel exterior. The center of the octagon held an arrangement of flowers. As I had not come across any building embellishment like this before, its uniqueness and its possibilities intrigued me. (Fig. 22.) The blossoms were composed of a variety of intricate petals and unusual shapes. If this design were to be used for appliqué, quite a few changes were needed in that portion of the design.

I drew the octagonal outline first to determine the amount of space needed inside for the floral motif. After much trial and error, and even more erasing, I eliminated the fine details in each flower and replaced them with some circles. (Fig. 23.) I still wanted a few flowers to retain some individual petals like the original piece, but there were too many to appliqué. I simply reduced the number of petals in some flowers and made the petals larger and easier to handle, something I should have done much earlier in the design process. As a result, my pattern still resembled the design on the building, but was now suitable for appliqué.

The name for this block evolved as I started to appliqué the pieces in place. The more flowers I stitched on the block, the more it reminded me of a pattern for dinner plates.

This pattern has a lot of pieces! I recommend it for quilters with some advanced appliqué skills. Appliqué in numerical order as shown.

Figure 23
Some flowers were simplified and others replaced by circles in the Bavarian Plate pattern.

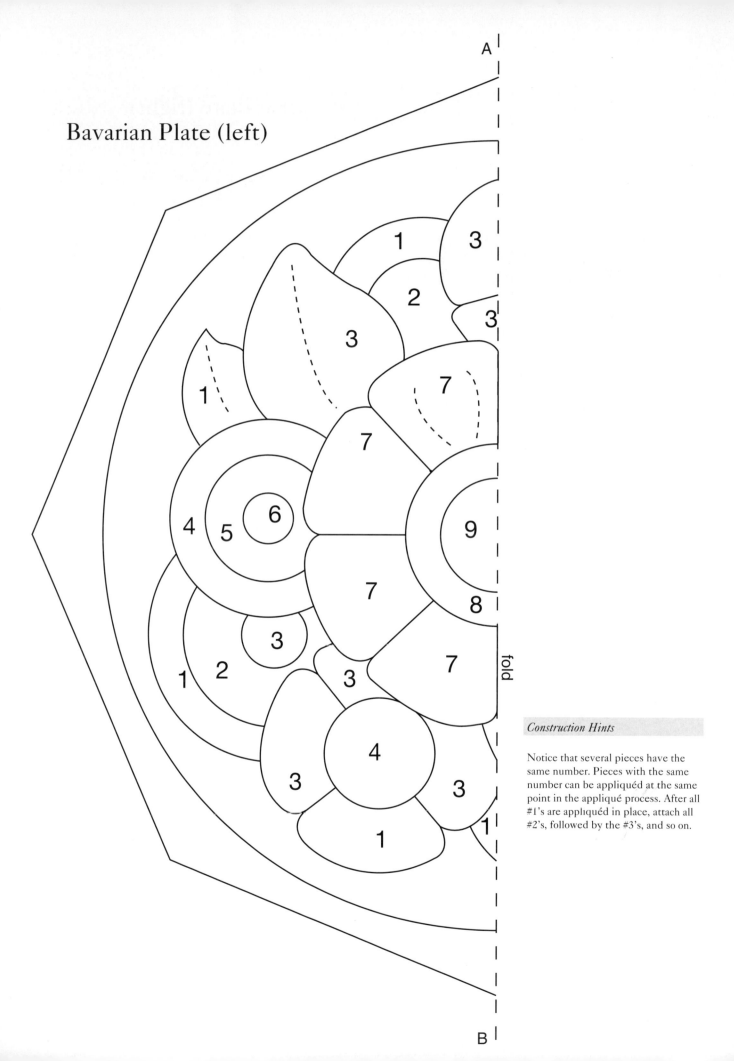

Bavarian Plate (left)

A

3

1

3

2

3

3

7

1

7

4 5 6

9

7

8

3

7

2

1

3

3

4

7

3

3

1

1

fold

B

Construction Hints

Notice that several pieces have the same number. Pieces with the same number can be appliquéd at the same point in the appliqué process. After all #1's are appliquéd in place, attach all #2's, followed by the #3's, and so on.

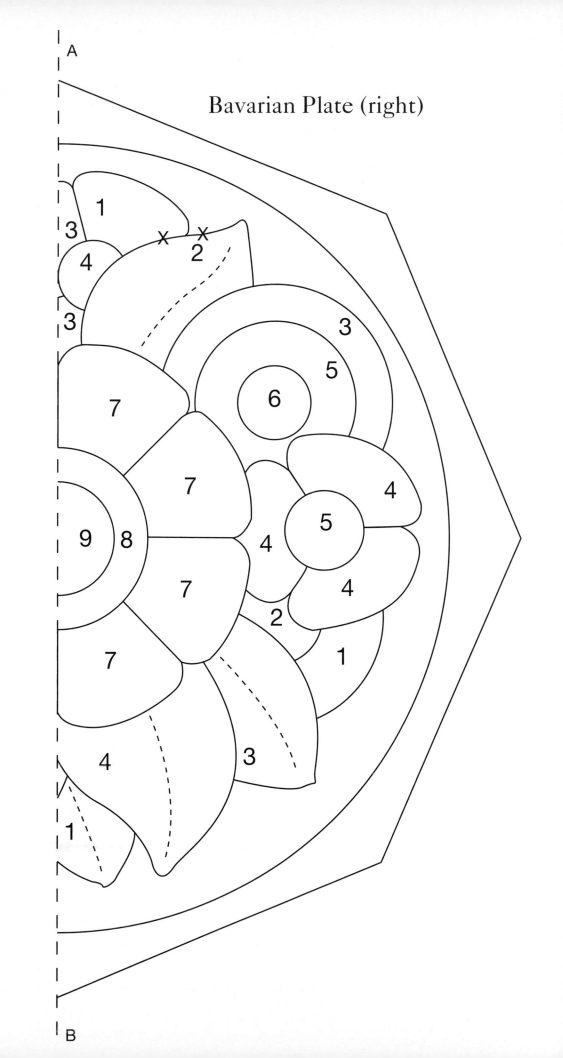

Bavarian Plate (right)

Bowl of Flowers

Frequently several architectural designs on a building are suitable for adaptation, and this design was also found on the same hotel in Milwaukee. (Fig. 25.) The blossoms were similar to those in the other pattern meaning they had too many petals or oddly shaped small details. This design would have been difficult to use in a 12" square without making some major changes. Quilting is supposed to be fun, not a lesson in frustration.

By omitting some of the flowers, I could enlarge some others. I then eliminated the petals by using five circles of differing diameters. By arranging and rearranging combinations of these circles, I created the illusion of a greater variety of flowers than there really were, and the general appearance of the original piece was retained. (Fig. 24.)

I made very minor changes to the shape of the flower container. Quilting stitches can be used to re-create some of the lines in the bowl.

The pattern is a little more difficult to appliqué, and those with beginning appliqué skills might want to keep this in mind. Appliqué in numerical order, but notice the circles have been given a letter also. Circles with the same letter are the same size. They will be used more than once in different positions on the pattern, and therefore it is unnecessary to make a separate pattern piece for each.

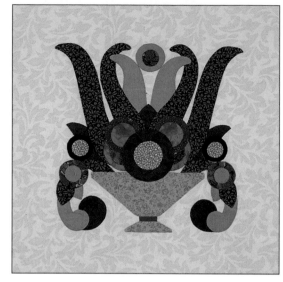

Figure 24
Circles replaced the tiny flower details in the Bowl of Flowers.

Figure 25
The arrangement of flowers and leaves makes this an unusual embellishment.

Bowl of Flowers

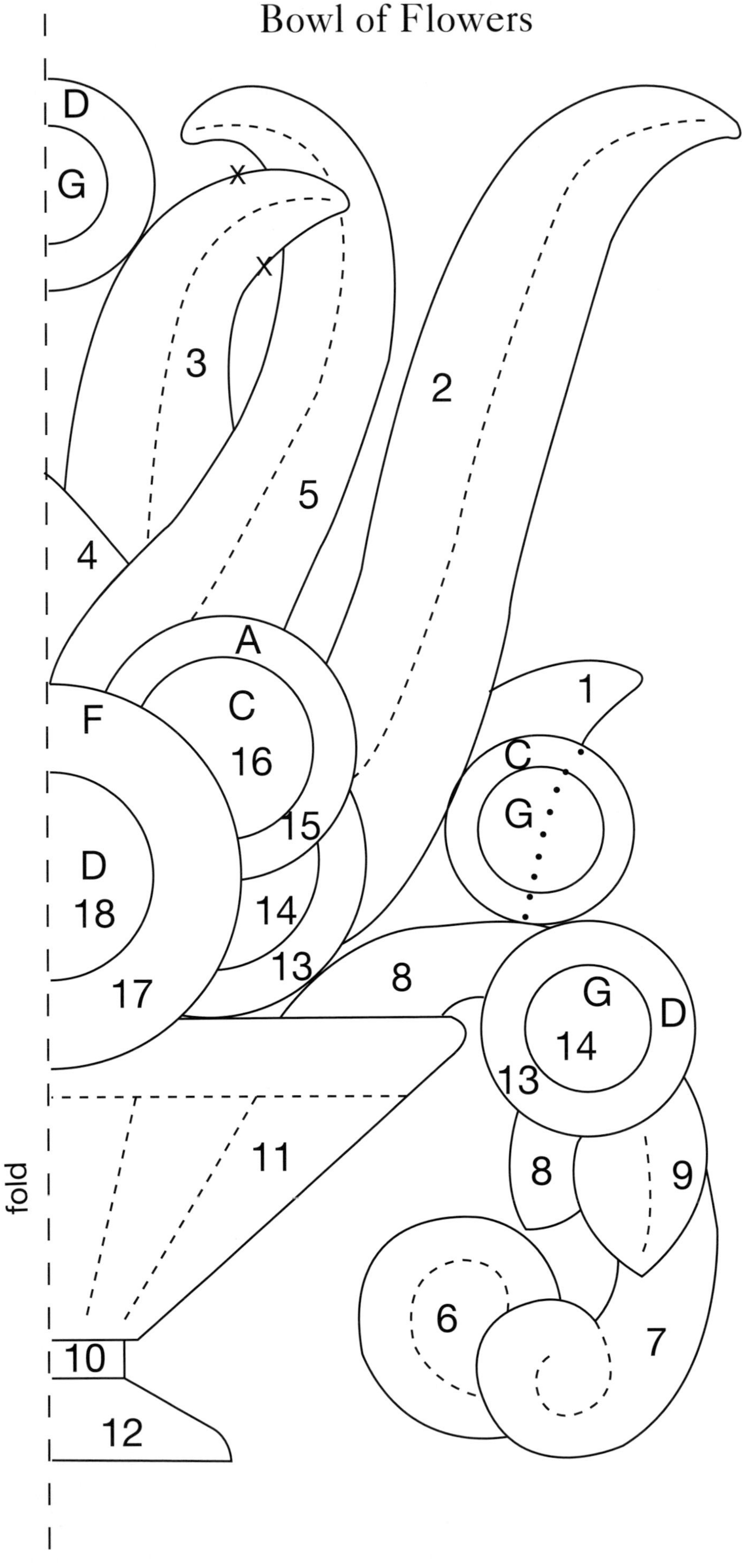

D

G

D

G

3

2

5

4

A

C

16

F

15

C

G

14

D

18

17

13

8

G

14

D

13

11

8

9

10

6

7

12

Construction Hints

1. When you cut piece #1, make it large enough to fill the space behind flower pieces C/G and #13 (note dotted line). The extra fabric underneath can be trimmed away after the appliqué is completed.

2. Pieces #3 and #5 (leaves) overlap each other Appliqué piece #3 as far as the "x," then appliqué piece #4 in place.

3. Appliqué piece #5 and complete the stitching on piece #3.

fold

1

CHAPTER 12

Filigree and Primrose

Figure 26
This panel of lacy motifs became a quilt pattern.

W hile on a trip to Minnesota's Iron Range, my husband and I visited a high school in one of the Iron Range cities. This part of the state may have iron mines, but the auditorium in this city's high school had a gold mine of embellishments! The auditorium was the most elegant I had ever seen. When the high school was built many years ago, the architect chose to duplicate the decor of New York City's old Capitol Theater for the auditorium. The Capitol Theater was built around 1900, and was reported to have been the most elaborate and beautiful theater in New York. Narrow vertical panels on either side of the auditorium stage were decorated with this filigree design which I thought I would try as an appliqué pattern. (Figs. 26 & 27.)

I wanted to retain the basic lacy quality of the original piece, but found it necessary to omit the flower shapes at the ends of the curls to make the pattern suitable for appliqué. The two thicker sections on each side of the architectural square were changed into thin strips of appliqué to connect the upper and lower halves of the filigree pattern. The flower in the center of the pattern duplicates the original.

Figure 27
Filigree and Primrose is easily recognized as a design from the auditorium panel.

I thought cutting and stitching all those thin twists and curls of the appliqué fabric might be like wrestling with a giant squid. There had to be a way to avoid the tangle of fabric. Using reverse appliqué proved to be a good solution to this dilemma. As the pattern is transferred only to the piece of fabric to be appliquéd, it is unnecessary to mark the foundation fabric. Reverse appliqué was also used to stitch the thin lines in the center flower.

Appliqué in numerical order as shown. I hope you are not scared away by the lengthy construction hints because this really is an easy pattern to do! The preparation time spent in basting will prove a big time saver when you appliqué.

Figure 28
The stencil transfers the pattern into each quarter of the appliqué fabric.

Filigree and Primrose

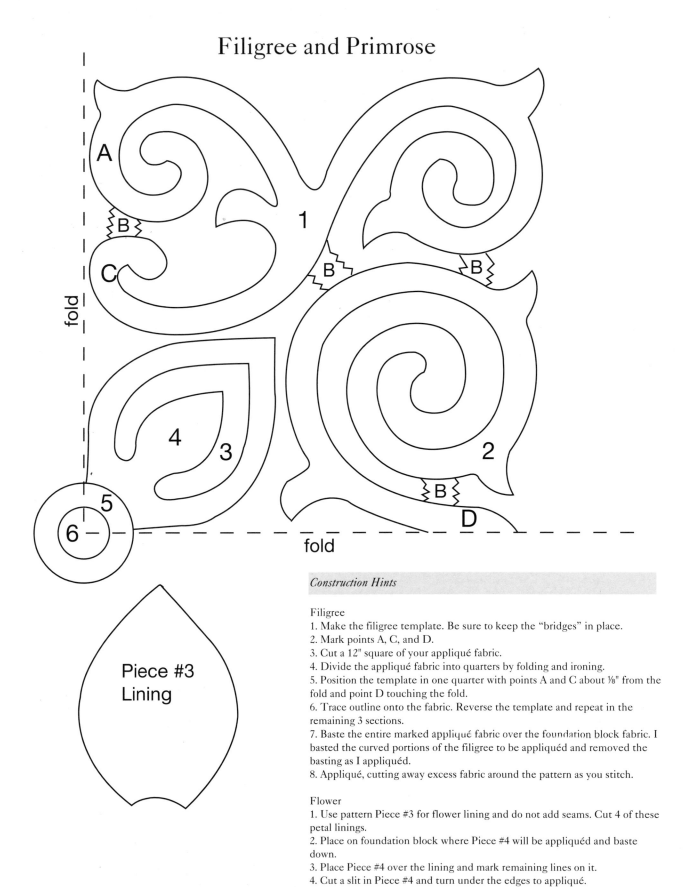

fold

fold

A
B
C
1
B
B
4
3
2
B
D
5
6

Piece #3
Lining

Construction Hints

Filigree
1. Make the filigree template. Be sure to keep the "bridges" in place.
2. Mark points A, C, and D.
3. Cut a 12" square of your appliqué fabric.
4. Divide the appliqué fabric into quarters by folding and ironing.
5. Position the template in one quarter with points A and C about ⅛" from the fold and point D touching the fold.
6. Trace outline onto the fabric. Reverse the template and repeat in the remaining 3 sections.
7. Baste the entire marked appliqué fabric over the foundation block fabric. I basted the curved portions of the filigree to be appliquéd and removed the basting as I appliquéd.
8. Appliqué, cutting away excess fabric around the pattern as you stitch.

Flower
1. Use pattern Piece #3 for flower lining and do not add seams. Cut 4 of these petal linings.
2. Place on foundation block where Piece #4 will be appliquéd and baste down.
3. Place Piece #4 over the lining and mark remaining lines on it.
4. Cut a slit in Piece #4 and turn under the edges to appliqué.

Swirling Leaves

Figure 29
Swirling Leaves was adapted from a small rosette.

The ceiling of the auditorium lobby at the Iron Range high school had a dazzling array of rosettes and moldings which reminded me of a quilt spread over our heads. (Fig. 30.) Lavish designs curled and twirled above us, and I knew an appliqué pattern just waited up there for me. Although several rosette designs seemed suited for appliqué work, two in particular provided the inspiration for quilt blocks.

One of the smaller rosettes resembled a cluster of swirling leaves, and I decided to work with that design. The rosette on the ceiling was three dimensional with the ends of the leaves curling under and disappearing back into the plaster cast, an effect difficult to achieve in two-dimensional flat fabric. My first few sketches looked as though the ends of the leaves had been chopped off by an extremely careless gardener, obviously not the effect I was after! Finally, I changed the shape into a full leaf and a small portion of it into a bud. The rest of the pattern remains much like the ceiling original. (Fig. 29.)

A beginning quilter with good appliqué skills should be able to handle the curves in the leaves without too much trouble. Appliqué in numerical order as shown.

Figure 30
Two quilt patterns were made from this ceiling.

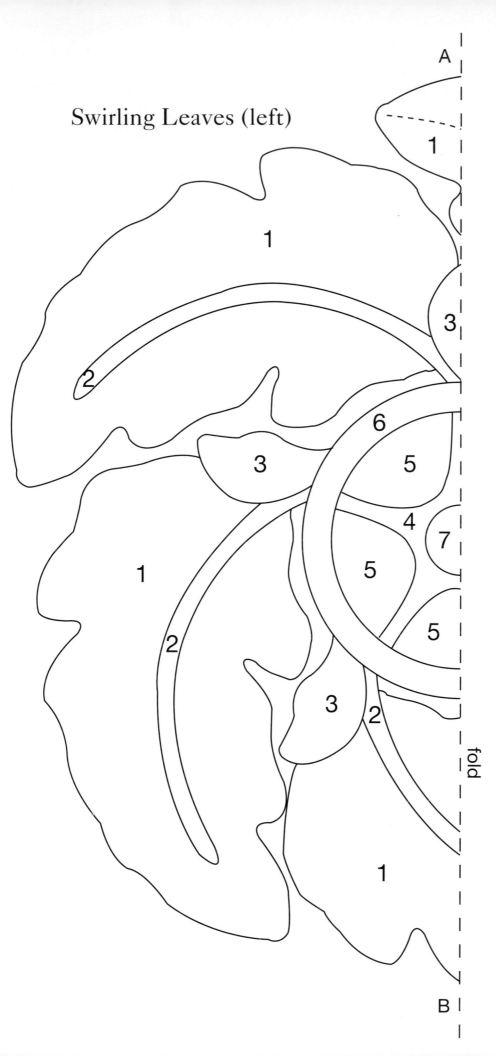

Swirling Leaves (left)

A

1

3

6

5

1

2

4

7

3

5

1

2

5

3

2

1

fold

1

A

B

Construction Hints

Center
1. Cut piece #4 just slighrly smaller than piece #6 to fit under the latter piece.
2. Baste piece #4 into place in the center of the pattern.
3. Appliqué pieces #5, 6, and 7 on top.

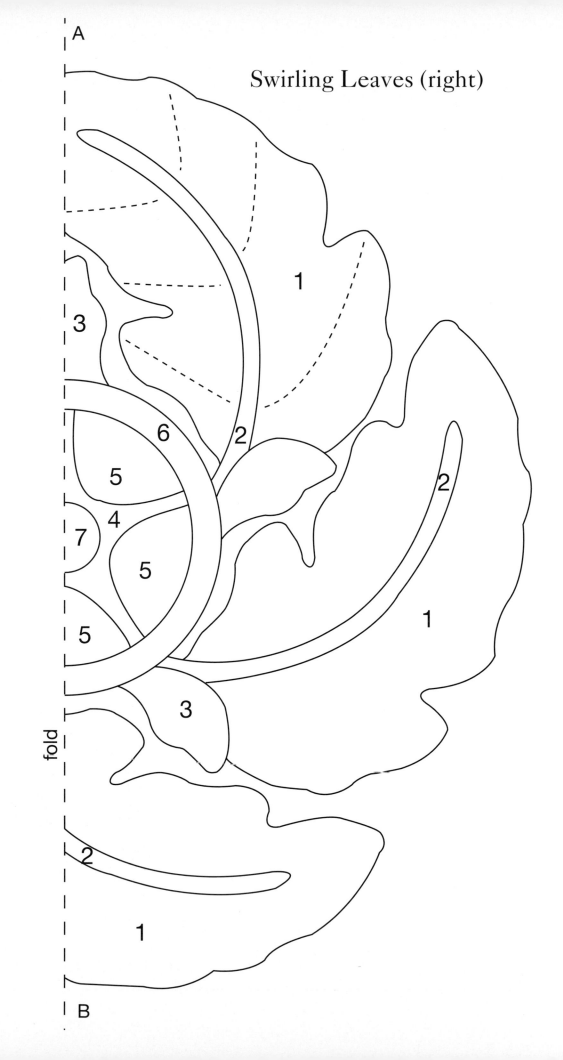

Swirling Leaves (right)

Interlocking Tulips

O ne of the larger rosettes on the lobby ceiling inspired the second pattern. (Fig. 32.) Within this rosette design, I saw eight tulips, each connected to its neighbor and circling a common center. I decided to work with this design and to try to make the tulips more recognizable to the viewer.

To begin the drawing, I divided a large circle into eight 45 degree sections, and drew a tulip in one section. When satisfied with the drawing, I traced it into each remaining section. To achieve the illusion of eight tulips, I let the foundation fabric show between the tulips and the center circle as shown in the picture of the appliquéd block. (Fig. 31.)

The center of the ceiling rosette was divided into sixteen panels similar to a Dresden Plate, which was more panels than I wanted to piece together. As the center circle still had eight sections, I used them for the center part of the pattern. For those who like working with small pieces of fabric, and who want to use sixteen pieces, divide Piece #3 in half.

This is an easy pattern to appliqué. Appliqué the pieces in the order given on the pattern.

Figure 31
One of the larger rosettes was adapted for Interlocking Tulips.

Figure 32
Two quilt patterns were made from this ceiling.

Interlocking Tulips

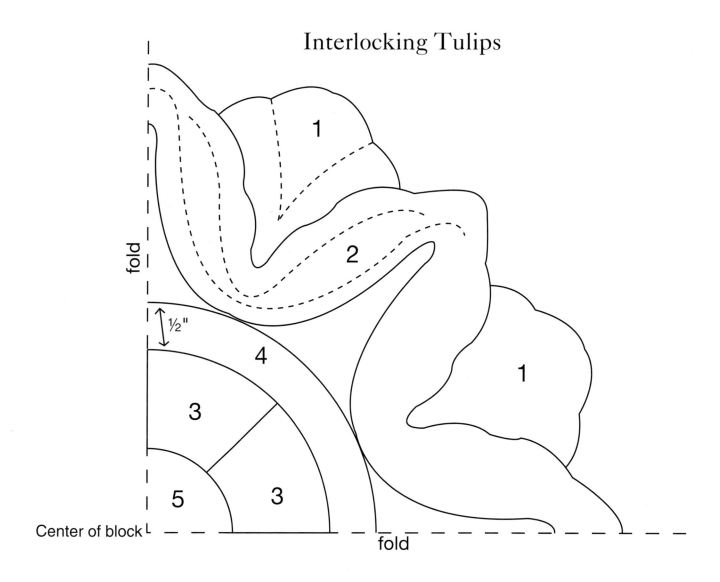

fold

½"

4

3

5

3

Center of block ⌐ fold

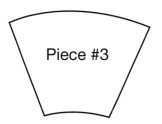

Piece #3

Construction Hints

Tulip Blossom
1. Cut Piece #2 from one piece of fabric. No seams please.
2. To keep the piece from stretching out of shape, baste it into position on the foundation block before you start to appliqué.

Center
1. Stitch the eight pieces together as you would a Dresden Plate constructing two units, each having four pieces. Then stitch the two halves together.
2. Piece #3, center of the pattern. Add seams.

CHAPTER 15

Star Flower

A public library in a Midwestern city has a floor made of mosaic tiles. The tiles are arranged to create a variety of star bursts, imaginative floral themes, and wild-eyed beasties. From this design assortment, I selected three that seemed well suited and adaptable for appliqué.

As this mosaic star design is based on a pentagon, I had to draft this geometric figure before starting any other part of the drawing. After drafting the pentagon, I drew a petal in one of its five longer points and then traced the petal into each of the remaining four points. The next step was drafting the second or smaller pentagon and completing the pattern by adding the five outer squares.

Each of the five petals contains a thin, spiky vein or point which would have been difficult to appliqué because the sharp angle creates a very delicate and narrow tip. I widened the points, rounded them slightly, and used reverse appliqué to stitch them. This solved the problem of the narrow point entirely.

The appliqué pattern for the Star Flower block closely resembles the mosaic design on the foyer floor. I even selected fabrics in similar colors. (Figs. 33 & 34.) The most noticeable change appears at the end of each mosaic petal where dark red and blue tiles accent each design tip. If I wanted to replicate the tiles, the piece of fabric needed for the tip would have to be very small. It was much easier to omit the tip as a separate piece and to make it one large petal piece.

The pattern is easy and suitable for all skill levels. Appliqué in numerical order as shown.

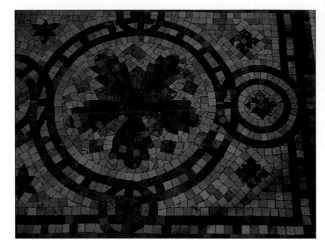

Figure 33
This mosaic tile design was one of several used for patterns.

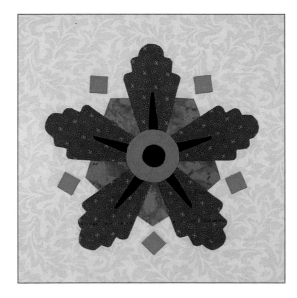

Figure 34
The appliquéd quilt block looks very similar to the one on the tile floor.

Star Flower

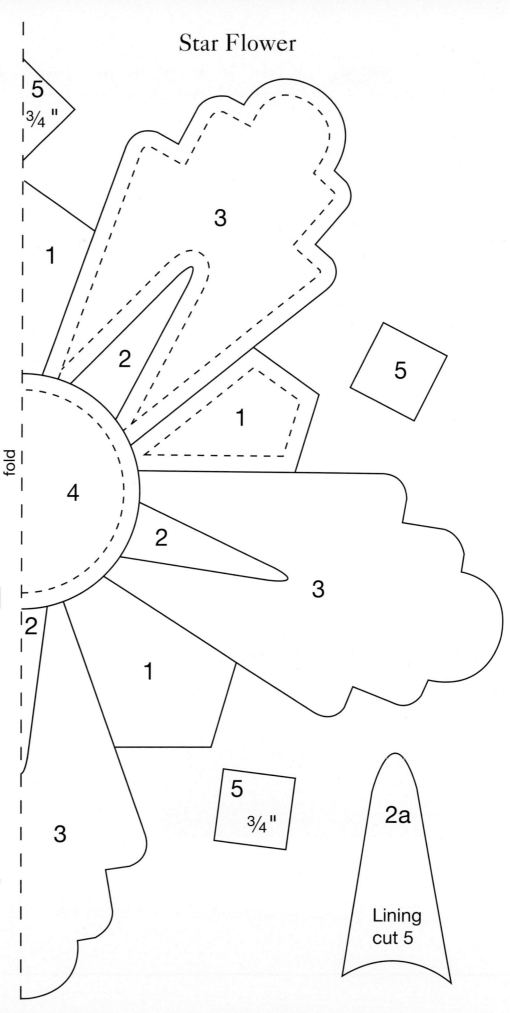

Construction Hints

Reverse Appliqué
1. After appliquéing all piece #1's in place, use pattern Piece #2a to cut five lining pieces. Cut these to the exact size given on the pattern.
2. Position the lining pieces on the foundation fabric where they appear under the large petal. Baste them into place.
3. Place Piece #3 over them. Piece #3 will completely cover Piece #2a at this point.
4. Appliqué Piece #3 in place.
5. Use the petal template, Piece #3 and mark the inner star point on the large petal.
6. Cut a slit between the lines just drawn. Be careful not to cut into the lining piece underneath.
7. Turn under the edges on either side of the slit and at the tip to expose the lining fabric and appliqué.

CHAPTER 16

Vase of Flowers – Variation I

rom the mosaic tiles on the public library floor, I also selected this design which is one of two unusual but similar floral
designs. I thought it would create a rather unique floral
appliqué. The design was taller than it was wide, and to make it fit
into a square, it needed more width. (Fig. 36.) I accomplished this by
extending the length of the buds, stretching them toward the sides of
the block, and stretching the curl of the handles toward the sides.
This helped fill the area within the square. I made changes to some
of the stems and buds and omitted a few other elements too small to
appliqué. (Fig. 35.) Simplicity is the definitive word when it comes to
adapting architectural gingerbread into a pattern.

Appliqué in numerical order as shown. Notice several pieces
have the same number which means they can be appliquéd at the
same point in the process and so on (#1's, then #2's).

Figure 35
Although several changes were made in the pattern, Vase of
Flowers–Variation I still resembles the mosaic design.

Figure 36
This is one of two similar mosaic designs used for a quilt pattern.

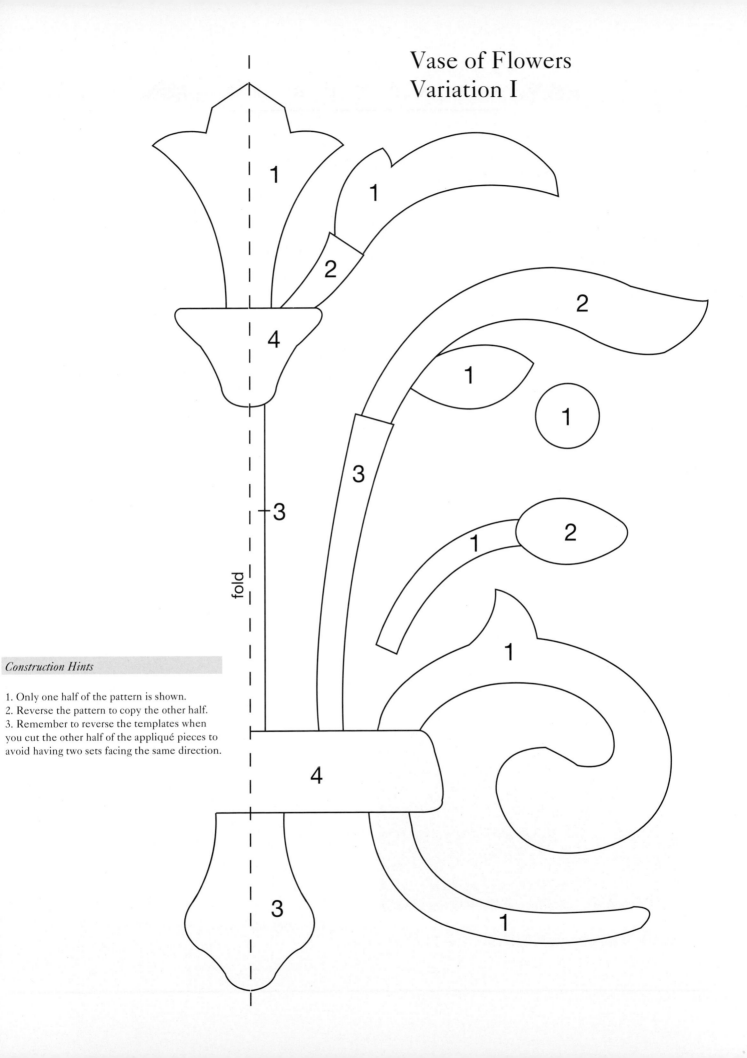

Vase of Flowers
Variation I

1

1

2

2

1

1

4

3

3

1

fold

2

1

Construction Hints

1. Only one half of the pattern is shown.
2. Reverse the pattern to copy the other half.
3. Remember to reverse the templates when you cut the other half of the appliqué pieces to avoid having two sets facing the same direction.

1

4

3

1

Vase of Flowers – Variation II

his design is the second of the two floral patterns adapted from the mosaic floor tiles in the library. Unlike the first design, it was wider than it was tall. (Fig. 38.) The tile designs were connected to each other by ribbon-like strips of tile which made this particular design appear even wider.

The first change needed was to alter the width of the design to fit it into a square. I did this by shortening the flower stems on either side which didn't leave enough space to include all of the remaining stems and buds. The pattern pieces had to be large enough to handle and stitch easily and could not be made smaller. I simply omitted some of them. An easy solution!

I made some major changes to the buds located at the ends of the stems. The mosaic tiles had gradations of color, and I wanted to be able to use several colors in my pattern, too. (Fig. 37.) Changing the shapes of the buds and making them a bit more realistic provided an opportunity to use more color.

Appliqué in numerical order as shown. Several pieces have the same number and can be appliquéd at the same point in the construction.

Figure 37
A similarity exists between the appliquéd piece and the original mosaic design.

Figure 38
This is the second of the mosaic designs which inspired a quilt block pattern.

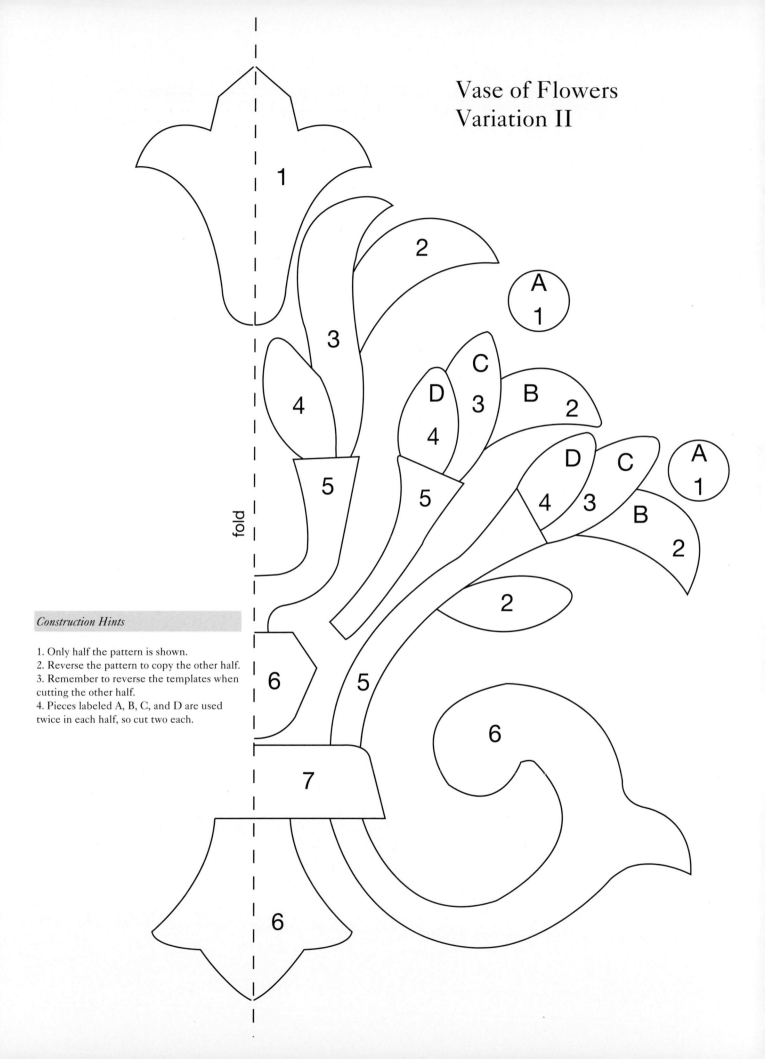

Vase of Flowers
Variation II

fold

Construction Hints

1. Only half the pattern is shown.
2. Reverse the pattern to copy the other half.
3. Remember to reverse the templates when cutting the other half.
4. Pieces labeled A, B, C, and D are used twice in each half, so cut two each.

SECTION III

Border Patterns

Rambling Rose

This border design is an architectural detail on the exterior of an old building in Milwaukee, Wisconsin. As the design was already laid out as a border, it was easy to visualize a quilt pattern. In fact, it appeared to be suitable for either appliqué or quilt stitching. An adaptation would not need too many changes from its original form and would not be too difficult to draw. I always consider the difficulty of the drawing whenever I work with architectural gingerbread. If the drawing is going to be too difficult, perhaps the pattern will be also.

Some of the leaves overlapped the vine (Fig. 39), and needed changing if the leaves and vine were to be cut from a single piece of fabric. After making those adjustments, I drew the pattern to fit a four-inch border. The pattern shown was planned for a four-inch by twelve-inch border length, but as I worked, I realized it could be adjusted several ways to increase the length. These are shown in the drawings, and the variations are explained in the following paragraphs.

Variation I (page 54). An extension of the vine at one end of the pattern simply can be made longer. Reversing the pattern creates a mirror image, and the ends of the vine will connect with each other. To continue the pattern, reverse it again so the curled ends with the flower in the loop face each other. Continue reversing the pattern to achieve the desired length. Additional length can also be added by increasing the space between the pattern repeats.

Variation 2. Adding an additional flower will also lengthen the pattern. Extend the vine as explained in variation 1 and add a flower between those two sections. In variation 3, the vine extension was cut away and the vine curved up and into the leaf. A flower can be appliquéd between these sections allowing you to adjust the space between them.

Appliqué in numerical order given. Please notice the flower overlaps the edge of the vine just slightly.

I have shown the appliqué version of this pattern in Figure 40, but it can also be used for quilted stitches in a border. Make a stencil by tracing the pattern on a piece of plastic template material or cardboard. (Fig. 41.) Mark the pattern on the border of the quilt with your favorite marking tool.

Figure 39
With a few changes, this building detail could be either an
appliquéd or quilted border.

Figure 40
Appliqué was used for this version of the pattern.

Figure 41
This stencil is used to mark the border on a quilt top.

Rambling Rose

Variation #1

Variation #2

Variation #3

Rambling Rose

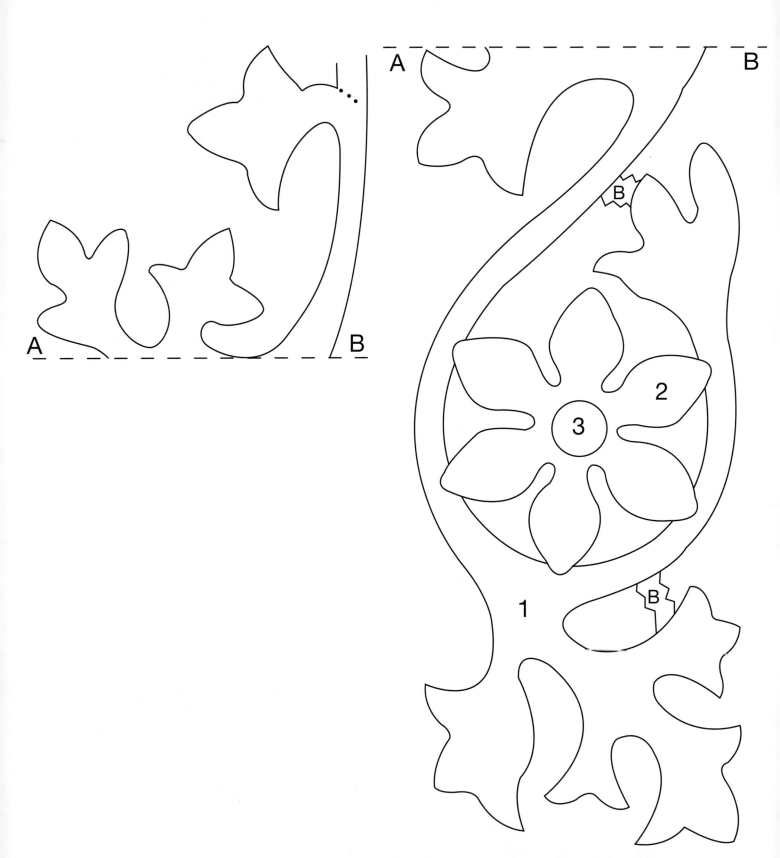

CHAPTER 19

Oak Leaves and Acorns

Figure 42
The decorative design of oak leaves is located at the entrance to a courthouse.

I found a very attractive border design around a doorway. Doorways seem to be good places to find designs suitable for quilt patterns. The graceful curves of the leaves attracted my attention because this design could be used without significant changes. (Fig. 42.) I needed only to make a drawing of the design to have a pattern for either a quilted border or perhaps an appliqué border. (Fig. 43.) What seems an easy enough task does not always go as smoothly as anticipated.

After spending an evening sketching and doodling, I could not get the leaves drawn to the right size or at the proper angle to connect and make a smooth repeat of the pattern. Then I had an idea! Why not project the slide of that particular design onto a sheet of paper taped to the wall? I adjusted the projector until the leaves were the size I wanted, then I traced a unit of one leaf, stem, and acorn cluster. After cutting out this drawing, I traced it onto a piece of graph paper, flipping the cutout as necessary to continue the pattern. I also made a few minor changes to the stem, and acorns at this point. This was so easy and accurate, I wondered why I had not thought of using the slide projector earlier, much earlier, in the evening.

The pattern shown will fit into a three inch wide border. Quilters are frequently unsure how to handle the corners of the border where the sides and ends meet. They will have no problem with this pattern. (Fig. 42.) In architecture, the problem was handled by extending the stem on the top border and setting it at a right angle to a leaf on the side border. This can be done with the borders on a quilt, too.

Figure 43
Use this stencil to mark the Oak Leaves and Acorn pattern on a quilt.

Oak Leaves and Acorns

Overlap the pattern on the dots to repeat the pattern.

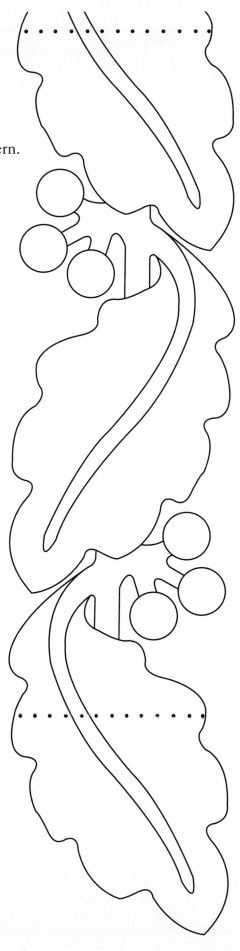

CHAPTER 20

Paths in the Garden

This decorative border was also found in the Iron Range high school auditorium and needed very little simplification to make it into a quilted border pattern. I just eliminated the circle in the small diamond shape. In the original, where the borders met and turned at the corner, the ovals ran right into the corner square, cutting off their tips. (Fig. 44.) Most quilters feel it looks awkward to cut off part of a border pattern, as though enough space had not been left to finish it. When I adapted the design, I completed the pointed tips of the oval. I thought it looked much neater if a full oval touched the corner square instead of a partial one. No pattern is given for the corner square because it can be quilted directly on the quilt without difficulty. Make the sides of the square the same width as the curves of the oval, ½". The flower pattern has been provided.

The stencil for this pattern is quite easy to make. Take a close look at the photo of the stencil and the pattern and notice a "B" printed between the lines. The lines are bridges and their purpose is described at the beginning of the book. When you cut the pattern out of your plastic or cardboard, be sure to leave bridges between the flower and the inner edges of the oval.

If you find it too difficult to cut the oval and flower section of this pattern, make the stencil in two pieces. (Fig. 45.) Make one stencil for the diamond and oval shapes and a second stencil for the flower. To mark your quilt border, first trace the diamond and oval stencil on the fabric, then place the flower stencil into position in the oval and trace its outline.

The dots at both ends of the pattern indicate how far to overlap the stencil when you trace it onto your quilt. You may find it helpful to mark the dots on your stencil. This pattern is four inches high and will fit into a five-inch border.

Figure 44
One of the designs in the auditorium is ideal for a border pattern.

Figure 45
Either of these stencils can be used to mark the pattern on the quilt top.

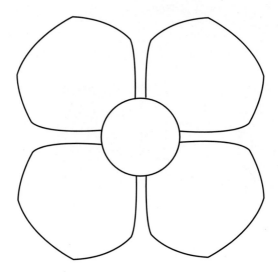

Pattern for the corner flower.

Overlap the pattern on the dots to repeat the pattern.

Paths in the Garden

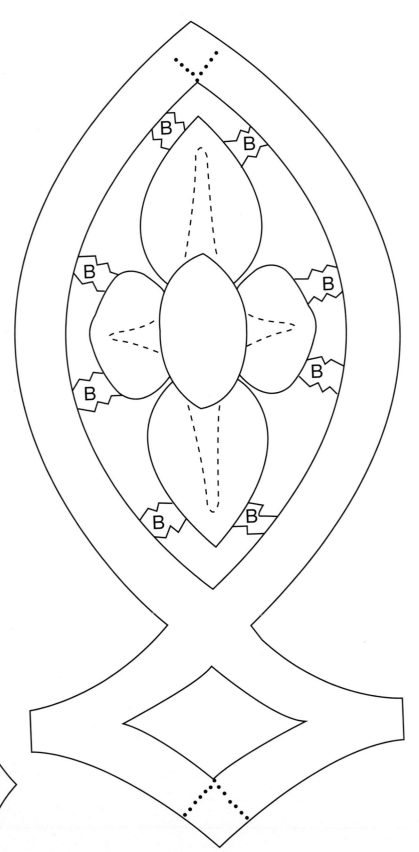

Lace Tulip

Figure 46
This architectural design will need to be simplified.

Many older buildings seem to have some sort of decorative work near their entrances. This is another design found around a doorway. It looked like it had pattern possibilities for a quilted border. (Fig. 46.)

As I started to doodle with the piece, I omitted some parts of the original piece from my pattern, primarily to make the stencil easier to cut. When the shape between the loops was left out, the outline of the tulip emerged. The tulip was made more visible after erasing the arched shapes at the base of the design. This was all well and good, but I did not know what to do where the two borders met at the corner. Some corners can be turned easily with the addition of a flower or the bend of a stem. In this case, the edges of the tulips ended abruptly at the corner. It may have been all right to use that way, but I decided to connect them by adding the corner curve. This simple solution turned the pattern into an attractive lacy frame. (Fig. 47.) Because of its appearance, I selected Lace Tulips as the name for the pattern.

The pattern given was designed to fit into a 3½" or 4" wide border. However, if you want to enlarge or reduce it, try photocopying the pattern.

Figure 47
The stencil for lace tulip.

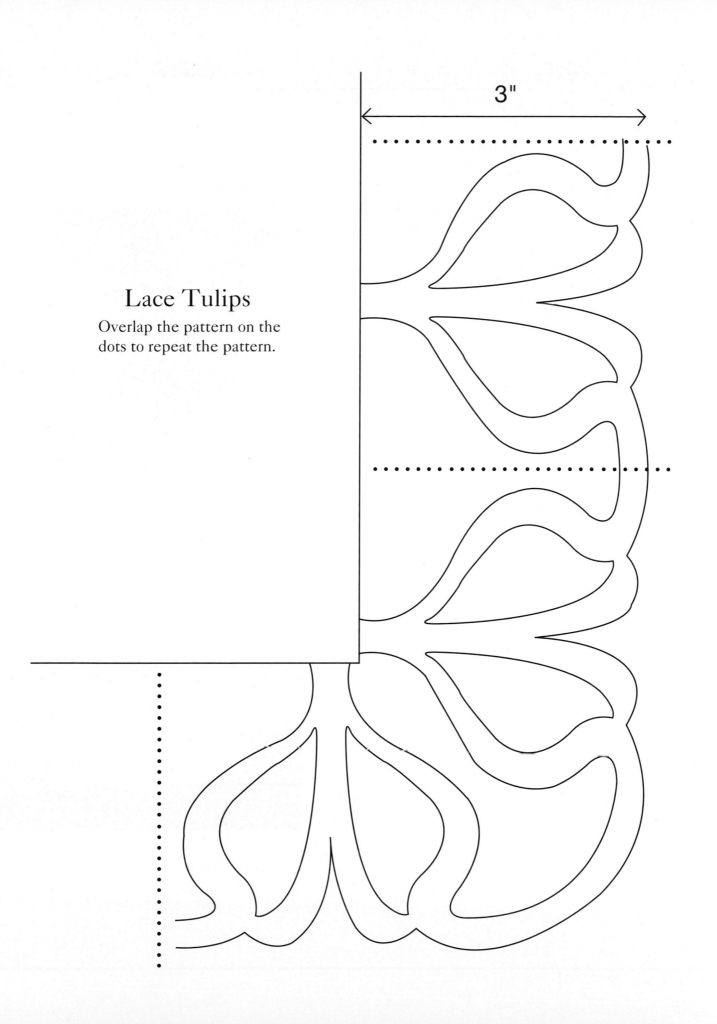

Lace Tulips

Overlap the pattern on the dots to repeat the pattern.

3"

Leaves and Scallops

A friend of mine has collected an assortment of carved wood moldings, corbels, fretwork, and other odds and ends of woodwork salvaged from old buildings. While visiting her home and oh-h-ing and ah-h-ing over these pieces, my attention was drawn to a piece of carved walnut molding. It was a perfect pattern for a quilted border and would need very little adaptation to make it suitable for that use. (Fig. 48.)

The straight edge of the architectural trim would line up nicely along the edges of the quilt's borders, and the scallops and leaves would create an unusual stitched design. The stencil would be quite easy to make, a definite bonus! (Fig. 49.) I eliminated only the vertical lines in the smaller scallop which you can see by comparing the photograph of the wood trim to the pattern. I then brought up the lower edge of the curve to make it the same width as the other scallop in the pattern.

The pattern is 3½" from the base to the highest part of the curve making it fit nicely into a four or five inch border. Dotted lines on the pattern enable you to position the stencil accurately as you mark the length.

Figure 48
A piece of molding salvaged from a Victorian home inspired the Leaves and Scallop pattern.

Figure 49
This is the border stencil for Leaves and Scallops.

Leaves and Scallops

Overlap the pattern on the dots
to repeat the pattern.

Cut away areas indicated
with an "x."

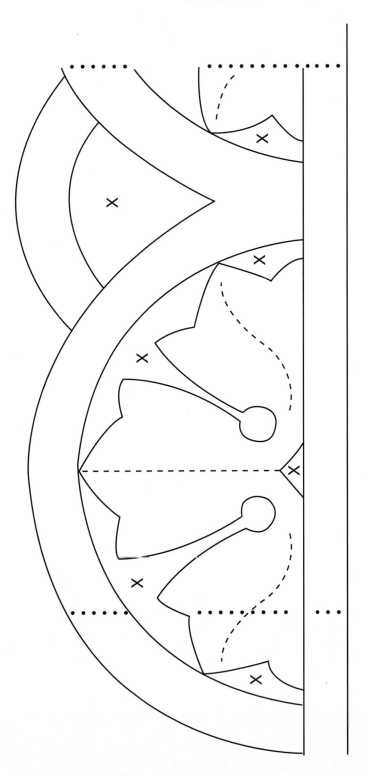

Daisy Spray

Figure 50
A carving like this makes a good border pattern.

This wood carving was located at the base of a door frame at the same history center where I found the oak newel post. The design was located just a few inches above the floor, making me wonder how many people ever noticed it. (Fig. 50.) Those who did would probably never envision it as a pattern for a quilt border.

The rectangular shape lent itself very well for a border. As the original carving was already quite simple, I made no significant changes to it. I wanted to retain the general shape and appearance of the carving when I made the pattern.

The stencil is easy to cut out as a silhouette. (Fig. 51.) It can be pinned or taped to the quilt top for marking. The lines forming the sides of the petals do not need to be marked before quilting. In the same way, the lines in the leaves, at the base of the notches, can also be quilted freehand, (or should I say freeneedle). I did not deepen the notches in the leaves on the pattern, to have done so would have weakened the stencil when it is cut.

The problem at the corner where two borders meet is easily solved with this pattern. Place a flower in the corner so each end of the border will start with another leaf.

The pattern could also be used as the quilted design on a block. Enlarge the pattern somewhat for use in a twelve-inch square by adding ½" to each stem as shown on the pattern and by placing the stencil diagonally across the square to trace the outline. Finally, rotate the pattern one quarter turn and trace the other two leaves on the diagonal.

Figure 51
Place this silhouette stencil end-to-end to mark the pattern on the quilt top.

Daisy Spray

Place the stencil diagonally to transfer the pattern on to the square.

fold

Center of block

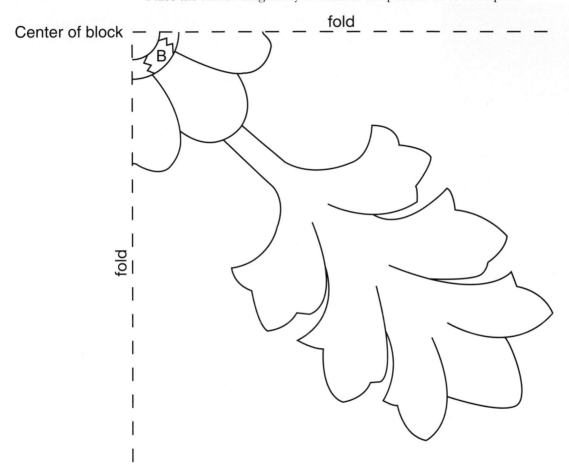

fold

Daisy Spray
Shorten or lengthen on dotted lines.

B

B

ABOUT THE AUTHOR

Carol Wagner is a native of the Midwest. She was born in Milwaukee, Wisconsin, where she later earned her degree in art education from the University of Wisconsin-Milwaukee.

Carol made her first quilt in 1974, "as an attempt to use up the years of accumulated scraps I had saved from sewing." That very first quilt proved to be the start of her fascination with quilting and its numerous possibilities as a means of artistic expression.

She started to teach quilt classes in her community in the early 1980's and later became a National Quilting Association Certified Teacher. She now teaches and lectures to guilds across the United States, and has taught at the American Quilter's Society Show in Paducah, Kentucky, and Quilt Festival in Houston, Texas. Carol does some free-lance writing and designing for quilt magazines and needlework books. Her articles have appeared in the *American Quilter, Quilting Today, Quilt World,* and some of her cartoons have been published in *Quilter's Newsletter Magazine.*

Carol's fascination with architectural gingerbread as inspiration for quilt patterns lead her to write her first book, *Adapting Architectural Details for Quilts.* This is her second book on this subject.

Her quilts have received awards in local and national shows and competitions. In 1986, Carol's quilt, Freedom to Dream, was selected as the winning entry from Minnesota at the Great American Quilt Festival, the nationwide competition celebrating the Statue of Liberty's 100th birthday.

Carol and her family have been residents of Minnesota since 1964. She and her husband, Howard, reside in a suburb of St. Paul.

∾American Quilter's Society∾
dedicated to publishing books for today's quilters

The following AQS publications are currently available:

- **Adapting Architectural Details for Quilts,** Carol Wagner, #2282: AQS, 1992, 88 pages, softbound, $12.95
- **American Beauties: Rose & Tulip Quilts,** Gwen Marston & Joe Cunningham, #1907: AQS, 1988, 96 pages, softbound, $14.95
- **Appliqué Designs: My Mother Taught Me to Sew,** Faye Anderson, #2121: AQS, 1990, 80 pages, softbound, $12.95
- **Appliqué Patterns from Native American Beadwork Designs,** Dr. Joyce Mori, #3790: AQS, 1994, 96 pages, softbound, $14.95
- **Arkansas Quilts: Arkansas Warmth,** Arkansas Quilter's Guild, Inc., #1908: AQS, 1987, 144 pages, hardbound, $24.95
- **The Art of Hand Appliqué,** Laura Lee Fritz, #2122: AQS, 1990, 80 pages, softbound, $14.95
- **...Ask Helen More About Quilting Designs,** Helen Squire, #2099: AQS, 1990, 54 pages, 17 x 11, spiral-bound, $14.95
- **Award-Winning Quilts & Their Makers, Vol. I: The Best of AQS Shows – 1985-1987,** #2207: AQS, 1991, 232 pages, softbound, $24.95
- **Award-Winning Quilts & Their Makers, Vol. II: The Best of AQS Shows – 1988-1989,** #2354: AQS, 1992, 176 pages, softbound, $24.95
- **Award-Winning Quilts & Their Makers, Vol. III: The Best of AQS Shows – 1990-1991,** #3425: AQS, 1993, 180 pages, softbound, $24.95
- **Award-Winning Quilts & Their Makers, Vol. IV: The Best of AQS Shows – 1992-1993,** #3791: AQS, 1994, 180 pages, softbound, $24.95
- **Celtic Style Floral Appliqué: Designs Using Interlaced Scrollwork,** Scarlett Rose, #3926: AQS, 1995, 128 pages, softbound, $14.95
- **Classic Basket Quilts,** Elizabeth Porter & Marianne Fons, #2208: AQS, 1991, 128 pages, softbound, $16.95
- **A Collection of Favorite Quilts,** Judy Florence, #2119: AQS, 1990, 136 pages, softbound, $18.95
- **Creative Machine Art,** Sharee Dawn Roberts, #2355: AQS, 1992, 142 pages, 9 x 9, softbound, $24.95
- **Dear Helen, Can You Tell Me?...All About Quilting Designs,** Helen Squire, #1820: AQS, 1987, 51 pages, 17 x 11, spiral-bound, $12.95
- **Double Wedding Ring Quilts: New Quilts from an Old Favorite,** #3870: AQS, 1994, 112 pages, softbound, $14.95
- **Dye Painting!,** Ann Johnston, #3399: AQS, 1992, 88 pages, softbound, $19.95
- **Dyeing & Overdyeing of Cotton Fabrics,** Judy Mercer Tescher, #2030: AQS, 1990, 54 pages, softbound, $9.95
- **Encyclopedia of Pieced Quilt Patterns,** compiled by Barbara Brackman, #3468: AQS, 1993, 552 pages, hardbound, $34.95
- **Fabric Postcards: Landmarks & Landscapes • Monuments & Meadows,** Judi Warren, #3846: AQS, 1994, 120 pages, softbound, $22.95
- **Flavor Quilts for Kids to Make: Complete Instructions for Teaching Children to Dye, Decorate & Sew Quilts,** Jennifer Amor, #2356: AQS, 1991, 120 pages, softbound, $12.95
- **From Basics to Binding: A Complete Guide to Making Quilts,** Karen Kay Buckley, #2381: AQS, 1992, 160 pages, softbound, $16.95
- **Fun & Fancy Machine Quiltmaking,** Lois Smith, #1982: AQS, 1989, 144 pages, softbound, $19.95
- **Heirloom Miniatures,** Tina M. Gravatt, #2097: AQS, 1990, 64 pages, softbound, $9.95
- **Infinite Stars,** Gayle Bong, #2283: AQS, 1992, 72 pages, softbound, $12.95
- **The Ins and Outs: Perfecting the Quilting Stitch,** Patricia J. Morris, #2120: AQS, 1990, 96 pages, softbound, $9.95
- **Irish Chain Quilts: A Workbook of Irish Chains & Related Patterns,** Joyce B. Peaden, #1906: AQS, 1988, 96 pages, softbound, $14.95
- **Jacobean Appliqué: Book I, "Exotica,"** Patricia B. Campbell & Mimi Ayars, Ph.D, #3784: AQS, 1993, 160 pages, softbound, $18.95
- **The Judge's Task: How Award-Winning Quilts Are Selected,** Patricia J. Morris, #3904: AQS, 1993, 128 pages, softbound, $19.95
- **Marbling Fabrics for Quilts: A Guide for Learning & Teaching,** Kathy Fawcett & Carol Shoaf, #2206: AQS, 1991, 72 pages, softbound, $12.95
- **More Projects and Patterns: A Second Collection of Favorite Quilts,** Judy Florence, #3330: AQS, 1992, 152 pages, softbound, $18.95
- **Nancy Crow: Quilts and Influences,** Nancy Crow, #1981: AQS, 1990, 256 pages, 9 x 12, hardcover, $29.95
- **Nancy Crow: Work in Transition,** Nancy Crow, #3331: AQS, 1992, 32 pages, 9 x 10, softbound, $12.95
- **New Jersey Quilts – 1777 to 1950: Contributions to an American Tradition,** The Heritage Quilt Project of New Jersey; text by Rachel Cochran, Rita Erickson, Natalie Hart & Barbara Schaffer, #3332: AQS, 1992, 256 pages, softbound, $29.95
- **No Dragons on My Quilt,** Jean Ray Laury with Ritva Laury & Lizabeth Laury, #2153: AQS, 1990, 52 pages, hardcover, $12.95
- **Old Favorites in Miniature,** Tina Gravatt, #3469: AQS, 1993, 104 pages, softbound, $15.95
- **A Patchwork of Pieces: An Anthology of Early Quilt Stories 1845-1940,** complied by Cuesta Ray Benberry and Carol Pinney Crabb, #3333: AQS, 1993, 360 pages, 5½ x 8½, softbound, $14.95
- **Precision Patchwork for Scrap Quilts, Anytime, Anywhere…,** Jeannette Muir, #3928: AQS, 1995, 72 pages, softbound, $12.95
- **Quilt Groups Today: Who They Are, Where They Meet, What They Do, and How to Contact Them – A Complete Guide for 1992-1993,** #3308: AQS, 1992, 336 pages, softbound, $14.95
- **Quilter's Registry,** Lynne Fritz, #2380: AQS, 1992, 80 pages, 5½ x 8½, hardbound, $9.95
- **Quilting Patterns from Native American Designs,** Dr. Joyce Mori, #3467: AQS, 1993, 80 pages, softbound, $12.95
- **Quilting With Style: Principles for Great Pattern Design,** Gwen Marston & Joe Cunningham, #3470: AQS, 1993, 192 pages, hardbound, $24.95
- **Quiltmaker's Guide: Basics & Beyond,** Carol Doak, #2284: AQS, 1992, 208 pages, softbound, $19.95
- **Quilts: The Permanent Collection – MAQS,** #2257: AQS, 1991, 100 pages, 10 x 6½, softbound, $9.95
- **Roots, Feathers & Blooms: 4-Block Quilts, Their History & Patterns, Book I,** Linda Giesler Carlson, #3789: AQS, 1994, 128 pages, softbound, $16.95
- **Seasons of the Heart & Home: Quilts for a Winter's Day,** Jan Patek, #3796: AQS, 1993, 160 pages, softbound, $18.95
- **Seasons of the Heart & Home: Quilts for Summer Days,** Jan Patek, #3761: AQS, 1993, 160 pages, softbound, $18.95
- **Sensational Scrap Quilts,** Darra Duffy Williamson, #2357: AQS, 1992, 152 pages, softbound, $24.95
- **Sets & Borders,** Gwen Marston & Joe Cunningham, #1821: AQS, 1987, 104 pages, softbound, $14.95
- **Show Me Helen...How to Use Quilting Designs,** Helen Squire, #3375: AQS, 1993, 155 pages, softbound, $15.95
- **Somewhere in Between: Quilts and Quilters of Illinois,** Rita Barrow Barber, #1790: AQS, 1986, 78 pages, softbound, $14.95
- **Spike & Zola: Patterns for Laughter…and Appliqué, Painting, or Stenciling,** Donna French Collins, #3794: AQS, 1993, 72 pages, softbound, $9.95
- **Stenciled Quilts for Christmas,** Marie Monteith Sturmer, #2098: AQS, 1990, 104 pages, softbound, $14.95
- **The Stori Book of Embellishing: Great Ideas for Quilts and Garments,** Mary Stori, #3929: AQS, 1994, 96 pages, softbound, $16.95
- **Straight Stitch Machine Appliqué: History, Patterns & Instructions for This Easy Technique,** Letty Martin, #3903: AQS, 1994, 160 pages, softbound, $16.95
- **Striplate Piecing: Piecing Circle Designs with Speed and Accuracy,** Debra Wagner, #3792: AQS, 1994, 168 pages 9 x 12, hardbound, $24.95
- **Tessellations and Variations: Creating One-Patch & Two-Patch Quilts,** Barbara Ann Caron, #3930: AQS, 1994, 120 pages, softbound, $14.95
- **Three-Dimensional Appliqué and Embroidery Embellishment: Techniques for Today's Album Quilt,** Anita Shackelford, #3788: AQS, 1993, 152 pages, 9 x 12, hardbound, $24.95
- **Time-Span Quilts: New Quilts from Old Tops,** Becky Herdle, #3931: AQS, 1994, 136 pages, softbound, $16.95
- **A Treasury of Quilting Designs,** Linda Goodmon Emery, #2029: AQS, 1990, 80 pages, 14 x 11, spiral-bound, $14.95
- **Tricks with Chintz: Using Large Prints to Add New Magic to Traditional Quilt Blocks,** Nancy S. Breland, #3847: AQS, 1994, 96 pages, softbound, $14.95
- **Wonderful Wearables: A Celebration of Creative Clothing,** Virginia Avery, #2286: AQS, 1991, 184 pages, softbound, $24.95

These books can be found in local bookstores and quilt shops. If you are unable to locate a title in your area, you can order by mail from AQS, P.O. Box 3290, Paducah, KY 42002-3290.
Please add $1 for the first book and 40¢ for each additional one to cover postage and handling.
(International orders please add $1.50 for the first book and $1 for each additional one.)